Steppingstones to Financial Success

Book A: Awareness

Steppingstones to Financial Success
Book A: Awareness

by
Dana Pride

Illustrations by Jahla Brown

Everlasting Publishing
Yakima, Washington
USA

Steppingstones to Financial Success
Book A: Awareness

by Dana Pride

Cover & illustrations
by Jahla Brown

ISBN: 978-0-9824844-0-1

First Edition
Everlasting Publishing
PO Box 1061
Yakima, Washington 98907
USA

Steppingstones to Financial Success

Book A: Awareness

GOAL:
Get one thing out of this book: Become actively aware of your own money by tracking your spending

Why I Am Writing This Book

Financial success... does that sound wonderful to you? What does that mean to you? Is that one of your goals? If you have not yet thought about Financial Success as a goal, you should. This is a goal you can begin to work on right now. Don't wait until you get lots of money, because without a plan and a goal, you might never get it.

Do you plan to get rich? How are you going to do it? Is a relative going to give you a large sum of money? Are you going to be a professional sports player? Are you going to be a famous rap star or movie star? Do you plan to win the lottery?

Do you know anybody personally who has gone from being poor to being rich instantly? Do you know why your friends or relatives have not done that? Because it rarely happens.

Most people who work hard will make a lot of money during their lives, but they may not have much at one time. Have you ever heard the phrase 'living paycheck to paycheck'? This is when a person or family spends the entire paycheck before the next paycheck comes – which can be a financial disaster if an emergency arises or the paychecks stop coming.

What is Financial Success to You?

Financial success may be all about becoming a millionaire or billionaire. It might be having enough money so that you never have to worry about it. Or financial success might mean coming out ahead every paycheck and having enough set aside for emergencies and for fun items and vacations.

Fun Fact: The more money a person has, the more that person worries about it. Will someone steal it? Are people trying to cheat to get it? Are friends real, or do they stick around to share your money?

4

If you do not have a plan and a goal for financial success, you will most likely have financial failure. I would love for you to get started early in your life, on your own path to financial success.

TRUE STORY

A True Story

When I was growing up, my parents were married. I have only one brother. My dad worked, he had a good job, and my mom was a stay-home mom (they were called housewives back then). My parents didn't tell me how much my dad made, but I knew he got paid once a month. I didn't know how much our bills were, but I did watch when my parents sat down at the dining room table once a month, in the evening after my dad's payday, and pay the bills together. They had a paper with a grid on it that my dad had drawn with all the bills listed: house payment, car payment, electricity, phone bill, water bill, natural gas bill, garbage bill, and savings. They had the stack of bills that were due, and my mom wrote checks for each bill while my dad wrote the amount paid on each account on the grid. Then they decided how much they could spend that month on food, clothes and anything fun, like going out to dinner, going bowling or golfing, and on gifts for family members who were having birthdays.

I saw my parents working managing their money every month, so I learned what they were doing and why they were doing it. Remember, my dad got paid only once every month, on the tenth of the month, so if a bill was due on the first of the month, they had to save that amount until the end of the month so they could pay that bill on time. They had to anticipate how much they would need later in the month, which meant they could not spend the whole paycheck on the day my dad was paid.

(Side note: The money they were putting into their savings account was not money they would withdraw later in the month to spend or pay bills.)

BUDGET

Watching my parents managing their money like this taught me the importance of paying close attention to my money. As a kid, I didn't have a lot of money, but the money I did get for doing jobs around the house, and then when I was a teenager, babysitting, I mostly saved. Why did I do this? Because I saw my parents setting a good example, and I did not want to waste money. When I wrote down everything I spent, I could see how much I was wasting, how much I was saving, and I could remember what I was getting for my money.

My brother, on the other hand, is younger than I am, and he has always had a completely different idea about money. He didn't watch our parents managing their money by using a budget, or if he did see them, he wasn't interested in what they were doing. He often went with Mom to the bank, so his perception was "when Mom needs money, she gets it from the bank." He didn't understand about depositing Dad's check first. My brother didn't see how the check was divided into

categories, and that a portion always went into savings. He just saw her getting cash. So, without the advantages I had, of understanding about our parents using their budget every month, he has never learned how to budget money. Unfortunately, he still has the habit of spending all his money almost as soon as he gets it. Do you think he has a savings account for rainy days, or for something he wants to buy in the future? If you said "no," you are correct.

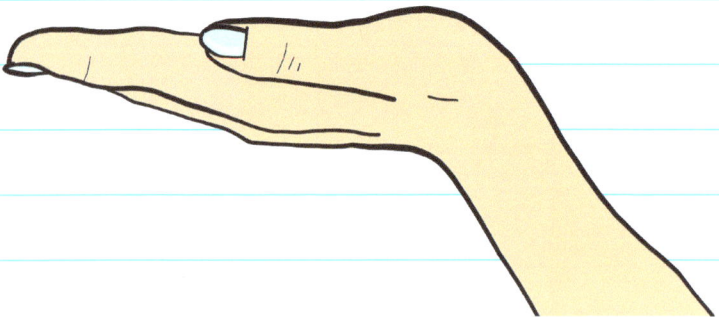

A real tragedy for teenagers – even in middle school – is that many are not taught the basics about money. Parents figure you will learn about it in school. Teachers hope you are learning about it at home. At school, getting into algebra classes and learning higher math is a high priority, to help your chances to get into a good college, while the importance of working with basic arithmetic and learning to make a budget is overlooked. I am hoping you will learn from this book how to become aware of your money: how much you get, how much you spend and what you spend it on. I hope you will put your knowledge to practical use, to start your journey in middle school on the Steppingstones to Financial Success.

BIG SECRET

What is the big secret about money?

People don't like to talk about money: Parents don't like to talk about money to their children. Why is this? One reason, they don't want to burden you with their problems. Why do many parents have money problems? Because they grew up not learning about budgeting and managing money. Most schools don't teach it, so many people learn about money by trial and error – mostly error.

Another reason parents don't talk to their children about money is because they don't want to share information about their finances. Most adults don't want others to know how much they make and how much they borrow – and, more importantly, they don't want others to know how much they spend, or how much they waste. In many families, the husband and wife do not share with each other how much they spend and what they buy.

Shhh...

Also, parents do not want their children to worry about the family finances. In addition, they could be ashamed or embarrassed that they are have so much debt and/or are barely juggling their income to cover the basics and provide the extras that children feel they should be getting from them.

Especially if parents are not telling their children how much money they **make, borrow, spend and waste,** their children, even children in middle school, need to learn the principles of having and using money: being aware of where their money comes from and where it goes, and how to save money.

TRUE STORY

True Story Number 2

When I was in Middle School (we called it 'Junior High' back then) I had a friend who smoked, and she always spent all of her allowance on cigarettes as soon as she got it. This was just about all the money she ever received. She was always intending to 'get more money' but she never had a plan on how to do that. So, she was always asking her friends for money or cigarettes, so they began to avoid her or they stopped being her friends. Even before she got started on earning her own money, she was behind, she owed friends money, and she did not know how **not** to spend all of her money. Since I was a money-saver and a good friend, I quietly pretended I didn't have any money either, so she wouldn't ask me for any; and I did not lecture her on how she should save some of her money and also pay back all the money she had borrowed from her other friends. Then she moved away, and I heard after high school she was not working or going to college, but she was living with her sister, who was working two jobs to support the two of them.

Don't be like my old friend. Get a handle on your finances now, while you still have a good chance to get ahead.

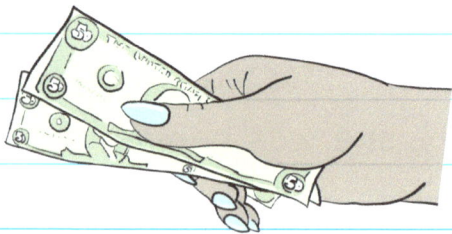

Becoming aware of your money.

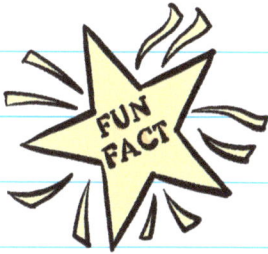

Fun Fact: Our memories are terrible when it comes to remembering where we spent our money – unless we write it down.

This may seem like a simple exercise, but it is very important. All I want you to do is to write down everything about your own money: how much you get, how much you spend, where you spend it and when. You can use a table like the sample on the next few pages, you can write it on paper (I recommend using a notebook to keep your pages together), you can create a spreadsheet on a computer, or you can download a blank form from my website. Spreadsheets are nice because they do the addition and subtraction for you.

If you do not know what a spread-sheet is, I advise you to look it up on YouTube.

Fun Fact: Did you notice I did not say 'spread-sheets do the math for you'? This is because addition and sub-traction are actually arithmetic, not mathematics. (You can look up the difference if you are interested.)

Bonus Download:

Blank Money-Tracking Sheet

https://www.danalpride.com/forms.html

GUESS ??
WHAT

If you find addition and subtraction to be too difficult for you, **guess what!** Your cell phone has a built-in calculator in it! If you do not have a cell phone, I recommend you spend the first $5.00 you earn or receive on a cheap calculator. You don't need a fancy one to keep track of your money, just one that can add and subtract. I am assuming you know how to use a calculator. If you don't already know how, watch a YouTube tutorial and learn how to use it.

Money Tracking Sample

Date	What	Where
July 1	Cleaned garage	Home
July 1	Washed car	Neighbor
July 3	Movie	Theater
July 4	Babysit brother	Home
July 4	Hamburger, fries, shake	Burger Ranch
July 4	Fireworks	Fireworks stand
July 7	Babysit brother	Home
July 8	Coffee	Starbucks
July 9	Movie	Theater
July 10	Gift from Grandma	Home
July 10	Gift from Uncle	Home
July 10	Gift from Mom	Home
July 10	Gift from Neighbor	Home
July 14	New shoes	Mall
July 14	New jacket	Mall
July 14	Digital downloads	Amazon
July 17	Babysit brother	Home
July 18	Movie	Theater
July 18	Popcorn, pop	Theater
July 20	New clothes	Amazon

Amount Received	Amount Spent	Category
$20.00		Work
$10.00		Work
	$12.00	Entertainment
$5.00		Work
	$11.00	Food/snacks
	$25.00	Entertainment
$5.00		Work
	$5.00	Food/snacks
	$12.00	Entertainment
$10.00		Gift
$25.00		Gift
$50.00		Gift
$5.00		Gift
	$72.00	Clothes
	$54.00	Clothes
	$10.00	Entertainment
$7.00		Work
	$12.00	Entertainment
	$7.00	Food/snacks
	$27.00	Clothes

July 20	Movie	Theater
July 20	Popcorn, pop, candy	Theater
July 23	Babysit brother	Home
July 25	Coffee	Starbucks
July 25	Pizza	Pizza Barn
July 25	Movie	Theater
July 25	Popcorn, pop, candy	Theater
		TOTALS

I went one step further and added up the Amount Received and Amount Spent columns. (Yes, I used a calculator). Do you notice anything interesting about this table for the month of July? Yes – more was spent than what was earned or received. This could be because the tracking was started with money already in hand – or something was left out. Perhaps money was borrowed. Borrowed money should also be included in your tracking, because,

	$12.00	Entertainment	
	$11.00	Food/snacks	
$8.00		Work	
	$5.00	Food/snacks	
	$11.00	Food/snacks	
	$12.00	Entertainment	
	$11.00	Food/snacks	
$145.00	**$309.00**		

unless it was a gift to you (which should also be included), you will need to pay it back. Writing it down will help you remember that you need to pay it back. In any case, write down **everything**. If you try to cheat by not writing it down, **who are you cheating?**

Looking again at the table, how much was spent on entertainment? How much was spent on food or snacks? How much was saved? How much was used to help others?

Challenge

Keeping track of your money may seem too simple and a waste of your time, but I can guarantee it will make difference if you do it faithfully. You will be able to see where you are spending your money and what you are buying, in addition to how much you are spending. As in the example, write the details of what you buy, such as 'hamburger, fries and pop' instead of just 'food' so you can clearly see what your money is buying you. Over time, you will know exactly where every cent came from and where every cent went. You can be the judge of your purchases: are you spending wisely or wasting your money? After 6 months of tracking your purchases and you see that you spent more than $500 on make-up or milkshakes and you

have saved nothing, you might want
to change your spending habits. The
important thing is, you will KNOW
where your money has gone. A terrible
feeling is when you just had several
hundred dollars a week ago and now
you have nothing to show for it. Did
you waste it? Did you lend it to
someone, or give it away?

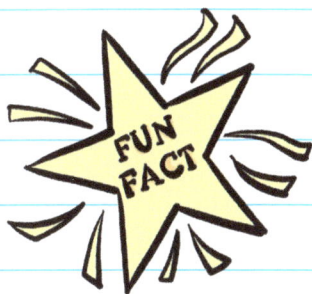

*Fun Fact: Usually when
friends borrow money,
they do not pay it
back. You should
pay back any money
you borrow, even from
friends: especially from friends.
But we will talk about borrowing and
lending in another book.*

When you track your money in a
chart like this, you at least will have
an idea of where your money went.

Challenge

Look over the table again. In your opinion, how much money in this table do you think was wasted? There are no wrong answers: this is your opinion.

Want vs. Need

You can cause yourself big problems by squandering away small amounts of money a little bit at a time. For example, you may think you need to buy a coffee every day. After all, you like the one that is only $1.99, and it helps you to feel awake and empowered. (I'm not sure why carrying a purchased coffee makes us feel empowered, but just holding that cup seems to make a person feel more important.) However, even if you live in a state where you don't have sales tax, $1.99 x 30 days = $59.70. (Yes, I used a calculator for this; it can do multiplication, too.) Do you realize you are spending nearly $60 a month just for coffee? Even if you save only half of that, after a year you would have $360 - and this is money that you literally drank as coffee every day.

This is where we discuss Want vs. Need. You may feel like you **need** to buy a coffee every day, but the fact is, you don't **need** it. You **want** it. You to **need** eat food every day, you **need** to buy school supplies, you **need** to do your homework. However, you **want** to buy coffee every day, you **want** to buy a new video game, you **want** to get every shade of nail polish available (or you **want** to get a manicure every month). In order to get yourself on the right track, on the Stepping-stones to financial success, you must admit to yourself what is the difference between **want** and **need**. Knowing this will make a huge difference in the amount in your bank account.

Challenge

Look at this list and decide what is a **Want** and what is a **Need**.

- Monthly manicure
- Video game
- Cute little toy
- Trendy shoes
- Pizza
- Fries
- Milkshake
- Coffee
- Latest fashions
- Winter boots
- Winter coat
- Latest Makeup
- Professional hair cut
- Notebooks
- Cigarettes
- Expensive sneakers
- Sports equipment
- Movies

- Fast foods/drinks
- Vending machine foods
- Smartphone
- Smartphone apps
- Concert tickets
- String lights for your room
- Laptop computer
- Airpods

Top items purchased by teenagers:

- Fashion
- Beauty and personal care products
- Digital media
- Food
- Video games
- Entertainment
- Savings

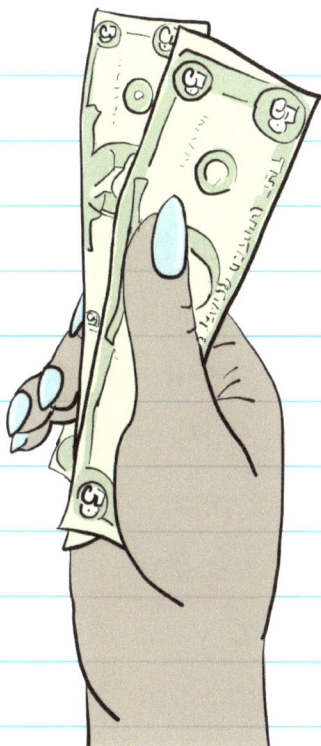

A Fool and His Money Are Soon Parted.

How important is saving money? Think of it as **paying yourself first.** Create a habit of saving. Put some of your money away, either hidden or in an account. (I suggest bank account, or, better yet, an account at a credit union.)

Very few people will support your decision to save money. Friends will urge you to spend it, to enjoy yourself, to treat yourself and to treat them. Why do they care if you have money? Because most of them do not have any, and they would prefer you to be just like them (or to spend your money on them.) Listen to your inner voice, the one that is telling you that **you** are the one who is going to make your future great; and one of the ways you are going to do that is by saving money every day. **Do not expect anyone else to just give you money. You need to do this for yourself.**

Challenge

Start saving money now, if you have any money at all. Put some aside. The next time you get any money, save some of it. You don't have to call it savings. Call it by the name of what you want to buy. When you call your savings by the items you are planning to purchase, the money doesn't seem like it is just lying there, waiting to be spent/wasted, or, as we used to call it 'burning a hole in your pocket.'

What do you want to name your money? **TIP:** You can save for more than one thing at a time.

A. Something Special

B. New Phone

C. New Shoes

D. Concert Tickets

E. College

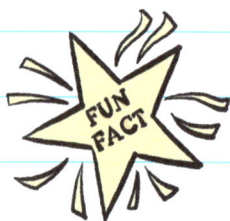

(Fun Fact: Middle School students who start a college savings account are more likely to go to college after they graduate from high school than those who do not have a college savings account.)

F. Rainy Day (Not a literal rainy day, but a day when you need to buy something and you realize you have the money saved.)

What you can do right now

Make money management a habit

- Know the difference between what you want and what you need.

- Thoughtfully consider everything you want to purchase (is it a want or need?)

- Pay attention to everything (write down) you buy (download that table)

- Learn how to save by just doing it. Start saving now. You won't be saving 'the wrong way' as long as you are saving.

- Put these steps into practice to form good habits

If you begin to form these habits now, while you are starting to earn and spend money, it will be easier for you to continue these habits throughout your life and you will be on the first step to financial success.

You Can

Challenge

What are the first **Steppingstones to Financial Success?**

- Think about money
- Be aware of the money you have and what it is for
- Thoughtfully consider everything you want to purchase (Will you be spending or wasting money?)

- Pay attention to everything you buy (write it down)

- Know the difference between what you want and what you need.

- Begin by taking one small step: Write down all the money you receive and earn and everything you buy.

I would love to hear from you. If you have been helped by my suggestions and techniques, or if you have any questions, you can email me:

danapride@everlastingpublishing.org

Or write to me in care of:
Everlasting Publishing
PO Box 1061
Yakima, WA 98907

BUDGET

Watch for the next book in this series:

Steppingstones to Financial Success

Book B:
Budgeting Basics for Beginners